# SEVEN DREAM KILLERS

Edited by: A.C. Bryan
Cover Design by: Geana Harris
Published by HRM Incorporated® – Publishing Div.
ISBN 978-0-9908788-6-5
Text Copyright © 2019 James Bryan

# ACKNOWLEDGMENTS

I want to dedicate this book to my wife and my family. Without my wife's love, support and push to complete this book, it would never have been written. Additionally, our children have been incredibly supportive throughout the process. It took much longer than expected but it is finally completed. I love you all!

***

I personally want to thank the Lord Jesus for revealing these Seven Dream Killers to me. The revelation helped me to soar higher and not fall victim to their strategies. My hope is you will be impacted in the same manner.

# Introduction

Life is an adventure— either we choose to enjoy every part of it or despise every moment of the trip. We can choose to mimic the child that says, "Are we there yet?" rather than experience the beauty and joy along the way. From my perspective, it is important not to miss life's adventures but to appreciate the journey while traveling to your destination.

Following your dream is an adventure: one that will take you through winding roads, the tallest mountains, and the lowest valleys. The journey comes complete with both expected and unexpected encounters with people of varying backgrounds and motives. A major part of this journey is choice— we cannot complete our journeys without it. It is important to think about this because everything we do is a choice. Our choices at each stage of our adventure matter. When one of our decisions brings advancement, it is possible to turn that into influence. God's intent is for you to succeed and advance!

One of my favorite Biblical accounts is the life of Joseph. Many of the situations and emotions he experienced are relevant to us today. Joseph experienced the love of his father, the hatred and eventual betrayal of those close to him, the feelings of isolation and abandonment, times of not understanding God, feelings of intense anger, a desire for retribution, acceptance and finally, restoration. Joseph went from cherished to abandoned to forgotten until he was finally fulfilled!

As you read this book, you may find that you are somewhere along this same path but have hope — fulfillment is on the way!

After having spent years in both the worlds of ministry and secular business, I have noticed tendencies among the successful and unsuccessful. These tendencies seem to heavily influence the outcomes of new business decisions, product offerings, new ministries, personal goal achievements and more. This book is not intended to place people in boxes or predict the successful versus the unsuccessful; however, it *is* intended to identify these tendencies and habits that prevent you from succeeding.

Over the years, I have had the pleasure to interact with people from all parts of the world, of varying backgrounds, and differing economic levels. Through all those interactions, it has become apparent that many wonderful and creative ideas are generated every minute of every day. These ideas are not dependent on a person's country of origin, their ethnicity, age or economic situation. If you have ever been in a room with creative people, you see each person thriving from the ideas put forth by the others in attendance. The result is usually a great product, plan or decision. Truthfully, in environments such as these, everyone is excited to come together to see what can be thought of or created next. In fact, some of the major companies that exist today are the result of people coming together with creative ideas to produce a wonderful outcome. The environment described is an ecosystem of success.

Without a doubt, I am sure you have seen numerous books in the store or online outlining the best ways to start a business— many of which are written about the successes of CEOs and how they became successful. These are intended to inspire a belief within the reader that they can also be successful. All these empowerment books serve a good purpose in that they energize our personal views about what is possible.

This book falls into none of the above categories and yet, in some ways, it covers all of them. I know it sounds cliché, but it is true. Although I will point to success stories throughout this book, my real focus is to highlight key tendencies that could cause you NOT to move forward with your career, position or life goal. These tendencies are often overlooked in the conversations, seminars and written material because they focus solely on the success but not necessarily on the hindrances.

When characterizing these tendencies or hindrances, I liken them to Assassins.

One day in 2012— I was a Senior Pastor then— while preparing the Sunday morning message, I began to remember several recent conversations I had had with different people. Many of them had great ideas about what they should do or wanted to do in business, ministry and life; and many had been discussing for years what they believe they are destined to do, but they never did anything about it. Oftentimes, they would say they had faith that it would happen, but they conveniently forgot that "faith without works is dead" (James 2:17). It was through these situations, that I realized that they all carried one or more common tendencies that prevented forward motion. Like any good minister, I used it as a teaching moment, and it became a series entitled, "The Seven Dream Killers".

At the core, these hindrances have a laser-focused mission intent on assassinating or severely wounding your dreams, your goals, and I would even say, your purpose! Because of the devastation that can be caused by these tendencies, I named them Assassins. These Assassins, left unchecked, will certainly slow progress enough to cause you to miss the proper timing for your destiny, therefore causing you to miss your purpose.

We must understand that all of us have a destiny, but it must meet the proper time in order for us to meet our true purpose. From my perspective, the concept of purpose is so important that we must all take a moment to understand it. I am convinced that everybody has a purpose in life; however, it is up to us to find it and walk in it. Although some would not agree with me, I also believe that a person's beginnings do not prevent them from serving that purpose. Therefore, I say dream big and find your purpose!

All God wants is for us to succeed and not get discouraged: there will always be opposition to you achieving your dreams and goals. Living an adventure that experiences no action, no advancement and no influence is what this opposing group would love to see in your life—don't let these opposing forces win. Within this book, we will identify each member of this group and provide strategies on how to turn what they mean for evil into good!

In the following pages, I will introduce you to these Seven Dream Killers. Some of the names may be those you expect, but others may be a surprise to you. Keep in mind that this list is not exhaustive, but it contains the names of key, repeat offenders. These Assassins aim to impact as many new victims as possible, without neglecting to continue suffocating the dreams of those they have already impacted. I would advise you not to cozy up and be friendly with these Assassins because they do not intend good for you. Avoid them and kick them out of your life. Your purpose depends on it!

# TABLE OF CONTENTS

Chapter One:     Assassin #1 - Laziness     3

Chapter Two:     Assassin #2 - Doubt     15

Chapter Three:     Assassin #3 - Distraction     27

Chapter Four:     Assassin #4 - Favoritism     41

Chapter Five:     Assassin #5 - Lust     51

Chapter Six:     Assassin #6 - Pride     61

Chapter Seven:     Assassin #7 - Unforgiveness     71

Chapter Eight:     Final Thoughts     81

*"Don't put off to next week what you **know** should be done today."*

# Chapter One
## Assassin #1 – Laziness

The first assassin is sneaky, stealthy and deadly. He is subtle, with the ability to impact outcomes before you know he is there. This assassin known as Laziness is there to cause you to lose interest, to always feel tired in the mind and body, as well as catch an attitude that says, "Oh, well. We can do this tomorrow." He is usually one of the first Assassins to show up on the scene once you declare you have a dream. Laziness may even allow you to get within close proximity of his target— even as far as seeing the finish line— so that he can kill and annihilate your dreams. In most cases, he maneuvers so close that it is nearly impossible to miss his target!

The arrival of Laziness is normally timed immediately after you have gotten excited about an idea *and* have made a decision to follow that dream or goal. All of us have experienced that wonderful moment when the "light bulb" clicks 'on' in our thought processes, and we realize we have a great idea. It is a wonderful time of clarity and excitement. In that moment, it seems that all time is standing still, the stars are aligned, and you feel that you are destined for greatness. The only thoughts that enter your mind are "Why didn't someone think about this sooner?" and "How quickly can we make it happen?" When I think about my own life, I have experienced numerous "mountain top" moments. In these moments I can clearly see the path to success, and I feel the energy of anticipation pulsing through my body. These are truly exhilarating times!

It's during these "mountaintop moments," that Assassin #1— Laziness— notices you and begins to target you as his next victim. You see, the problem is he knows we have to come down from the mountain and begin to work to make the dream happen. Laziness is not compelled to "climb the mountain" with you because he can wait for you to come down. He is content to allow you to have a few moments of exhilaration while he plans his attack immediately after you've descended the mountain.

There is a saying: "An idea without a plan is just a dream." I want your dreams to become a reality, so put that plan together!

I'm reminded of a Biblical account where Moses went to the mountain top to be with God for 40 days and nights. He had an indescribable experience in the presence of God where he could clearly see the path he needed to take; however, when he came down the mountain, he had to deal with people who didn't have the same vision or heart. In fact, the people made up their minds that they didn't want to follow God's ways at all. They quickly forgot all that Moses taught them —in less than two months! The vision, commitment, and enthusiasm were gone.

Moses' experience with his people is no different than what we face today. When we come "down from the mountain," there are many— will be many—who may not share your vision. Frequently, they may discount and ignore you when you attempt to cast your vision. These are the ones who can tell you everything that is wrong with your vision, but when you extend an opportunity to provide constructive alternatives, they do not have anything positive to say. These may also be the ones that mumble, "that's a dumb idea," or will be quick to tear you down. This is the beginning of Assassin #1 targeting your dream.

Once we come down from the mountain, we face the reality check. The reality being: those around us have not had the same experience or vision. It is at this point Laziness suggests that you delay the vision because it will be too much work— especially to get others to change their minds. The job of this Assassin is to make sure you take a detailed look at everything you don't have and realize the seemingly enormous task ahead so that you will abort your dream. To be dramatic, it is almost as if he wants you to take a long, slow look at everything in front of you and ask, "Do I *really* want to do this?" More importantly, "*Can* I do this?"

His timing is impeccable. He is drawn to every new and exciting thought or idea. Whether there is an invisible loud speaker announcing the birth of a new idea or goal, I don't know; he comes quickly so that he may put that new idea or goal in his sights and eliminate it before it can take root. His rationale is that it is easier to eliminate a dream or goal in the formative stages than it is after it has taken root. Once the idea has taken root, it is like an Oak tree that is deeply rooted and unwavering. These trees can withstand storms, hurricanes and other types of weather... and they continue to stand. Small, young trees do not stand a chance during a heavy ferocious storm; *that* is why landscapers often install wooden support next to the young trees. The hope is that these wooden supports can help the young tree stand long enough to take root. Like the other Assassins, Laziness wants to be sure your ideas stay a dream without a plan.

**Tactics of Assassin #1**
The tactics used by this assassin are well known and effective. He uses a long list of methods to deter you from realizing your dreams, making him one of the most effective Assassins of the bunch.

For example, let's say there's a person— we'll call him Joe— who attends a conference. At the conference, Joe meets creative people, who inspire him to form an idea to build a tutoring center for children in his city. He knows the city needs this kind of support because, as an educator, he sees the need every day. Joe realizes that no affordable facility of this type exists in his city. While Joe is at the conference, he encounters several people who have opened similar facilities in their cities. This boosts his confidence of success in his own city. Joe gets so excited that the night before his scheduled departure to return home, he finds it difficult to sleep. His mind is flooded with the images of the children he could help, the families that could be positively impacted, and that he could bring a major benefit to his city.

While Joe is up pacing the floor in excitement, Laziness is already on his way. Laziness is searching through his arsenal, deciding which weapon he will use. At this stage, it would seem that Assassin #1 has no chance of affecting Joe. Unfortunately, based on years of experience, Laziness knows he has a good shot at killing or wounding Joe's dream. How? There are a few ways.

Once Joe leaves the conference and returns home, he is anxious to take his dream to the next step. This is where Laziness begins his work. When he arrives home still overflowing with excitement, he shares his great idea with people he knows. Instead of being met with support, Joe is met with criticism. They point out all the potential approval and funding issues he would have to overcome, possible unfavorable outcomes, and even the difficult political environment in his city. By the end of the conversation, Joe's friends convince him to push off any decisions for a week— they tell him to *think about it*.

After a week, Joe finds that the demands from other parts of his life have taken priority. This causes him to push off any decisions regarding his dream for a month, and before Joe knows it, the month subtly turns into a year.

How did this happen?

Joe did not MAKE time to plan, so life's demands overtook him. His dream never turned into a plan, and unfortunately, it barely lives on life-support as slightly more than an idea. It is at this point that Laziness smiles, records the victory, and begins to search for the next target!

Is that the only way that Laziness works? Not at all! He has other tools in his arsenal. In an alternative version of events:

Joe arrives home, he calls his local government and inquires about the steps to officially setup his organization. They are glad to assist and send him documents and forms that are several inches thick. Joe looks at it, realizes that it will take an enormous amount of time and research to complete, so he delays beginning the work until he has more time. Truthfully, Joe gets overwhelmed by the volume of information and begins to feel exhausted before he does anything. He continues to tell himself and others about his dream, but he neglects to begin any actionable steps. Days, weeks and months go by without any measurable progress, but he continues to say that he is going to get to it.

> In the examples above, Laziness utilizes one of his primary weapons— **delay**. This delay tactic assumes that tomorrow will be a better and easier day to address what is in front of you now; convinces you that it will be no problem tomorrow and that everything will fall into place. In other words, Laziness attempts to convince you that all resources, open doors, and clarity of mind will overtake you tomorrow rather than today. This Assassin does not tell you that the longer you delay, the less likely it is for you to succeed. He doesn't tell you that over time, you are likely to forget the details of the idea, nor does he tell you that your resources may disappear as time progresses. He doesn't want you to begin your thorough analysis and planning.

Assassin #1 would prefer you to agree with J. Wellington Wimpy (aka Wimpy) from the old Popeye comic strip. For those too young to know, Wimpy was a well-educated, but lazy man. His favorite food was hamburgers and he would often say, "Cook me up a hamburger. I'll gladly pay you on Thursday." You see, he wasn't willing to pay the price now, but wanted to push it off to a future time with hopes that the time to pay the price would never come. This Assassin wants you to embrace this mindset. "Delay it as long as you want. The longer, the better." That is Laziness' mindset.

The subtleness of Laziness is really amazing; most of the time, we do not even notice his presence. He slows down progress until Joe, or someone else, releases their hold on their dream. He immediately pounces on the opportunity to take the dream and strangle the life out of it until there is only the slight memory left. Certainly, there is no action taking place to achieve the dream; which is always Laziness' goal.

To add insult to injury, sometime later (months or even years), Joe will see an advertisement of someone who decided a tutoring center would be needed in his city, but *they* built it. The advertisement will talk about the positive impact on the community, the partnership with the local government, and the positive economic impact on families because the children are better educated and landing better jobs. Immediately, Joe will shout, "That was MY idea! I was going to do that." Although Joe may have been the first to have the idea, he was not the first to ACT on it. Assassin #1 had successfully killed his dream. Now, Joe can only wish he had followed through and not listened to this Assassin.

➢ Another tactic of Laziness is to trick you into thinking that all resources will miraculously fall into place thereby, requiring very little effort on your part. He will even convince you to think, "I came up with the idea so everyone should do the work for me." Unfortunately, that isn't usually the case. The truth is, for any new endeavor, the originator of the idea must be heavily involved or the outcome— if there is an outcome— will not be what is expected. *All dreams require a "labor of love"* which Laziness does not want you to understand.

When I look at the Biblical account of Joshua's life, he was given the leadership role to take his countrymen into their dream— the Promised Land. This land was "flowing with milk and honey." In other words, it had everything they could ever want or desire— food, livestock, water, fertile ground and much more. Even with the gift of the land and its benefits, Joshua and his army still had to work to make the dream a reality. They had to move out people who didn't belong there; additionally, trees had to be cleared, homes built, ground tilled and much more. You see, that terrible four-letter word called "work" still had to be done. But the great thing about work is you appreciate your promise much more than someone who is not invested fully into the dream. It becomes a point of joy, not hardship. Assassin #1 would paint a picture of the work being too much for you and that you would fail, so don't spend the energy. For those who accept his argument, they experience a life that is unsatisfying and below their own expectations. This leads to disappointment and a cessation of dreaming.

**Strategies to Thwart the Tactics of Assassin #1**

As mentioned earlier, Assassin #1 does not want your dream to take root and grow. To counter his attack at the birth of your dream, you should take the following steps:

1. Write the vision – during your "mountain top" moment, make sure you write the vision in as much detail as possible. This will prevent you from forgetting important information once you have come down from the mountain. In order to do this, you must always have some type of recording device with you at all times. It could be pencil and paper or more commonly in today's society, a smart phone. I know several people who use their smart phone as dictation devices to record their latest brainstorm or idea. Later, they copy it to a more permanent storage solution. Once you have written or recorded it, review it a couple of times to make sure you haven't forgotten something. My personal experience is the longer the time period from the generation of the idea to the

recording of it, the less likely it will be that all of the necessary information is captured. In most cases, a partial dream does not live very long. Next, make multiple copies for yourself so that if one copy is lost or corrupted, you still have another. Whether you know it or not, God understands every tactic of Assassin #1. When speaking to Habakkuk regarding another incident, He told him to "...Write down the revelation and make it plain on tablets so that a herald may run with it" (Habakkuk 2:2).

2. Contact information – if others played an instrumental and supportive role in helping you come up with the idea, get their contact information. This is important because if you trust them, you may need to follow-up with them at a later time for clarification on various points. Who better to help you than those who were there in the beginning? Additionally, you want them to continue to be excited about the endeavor because they may provide additional connections you didn't know you needed. Also, they may do pro bono work since they are also interested in seeing the idea develop. Remember to utilize the resources already in front of you!

3. Accountability partners –identify one or more people that will regularly check in with you to

ensure you are making progress on a regular basis. Ideally, you would check in with this person on a weekly basis to ensure you are moving according to your milestones. If possible, you should have at least one accountability partner who has business or other knowledge that can provide value and advice to you. Accountability Partners will PUSH you to move forward to completion. They will not allow Assassin #1 to claim another victim.

4. Ask for help – do not be afraid to ask for help if you feel overwhelmed. Truly successful people recognize their own weaknesses and pursue help in those areas to increase the likelihood of success. To be honest, if you ask anyone that you consider successful if they had a moment where they felt they needed help, all of them would say YES, if they're honest. Getting help will also encourage you and inspire you to continue to move forward.

All four of these strategies cause you to make enough forward progress that Laziness will not have a chance to lock on and target your dreams. In fact, you will be able to resist all of his tactics so that you can run toward the fulfillment of your dream.

# Chapter Two
## Assassin #2 – Doubt

Crouching in the dark corners of your life, is an accomplished assassin that loves to provide an unexpected sucker punch to your plans, your dreams, your investments and your life. Like a snake, he slowly wraps himself around your very dreams aiming to disorient you. Once he disorients you, he relentlessly works to strangle your dreams and your goals— at times, working in conjunction with other Assassins. This assassin has had centuries of experience and is alive and well in the 21st century!

The problem in facing this Assassin is he can strike at any time. It could be early on when you're just beginning to pursue your dreams, or even at the point where you have almost achieved your goals. One thing is certain— he patiently waits for the opportune time to strike. Therefore, we must always be cognizant of his whereabouts and tactics. Doubt's impact is dramatic and dangerous.

Imagine a car racing down a track. As it barrels faster and faster down the track, it gets closer to the finish line; but, suddenly, dozens of parachutes unexpectedly deploy from the car— ultimately slowing down progress. Instead of accelerating to over 200 mph, the parachutes have caused your speed to drop down to an unimpressive 40 mph!

Even still, additional parachutes are deployed resulting in an even slower forward momentum. Eventually, the car will come to a complete stop; even if it works harder to regain the speed it lost when the parachutes were deployed. Doubt works the same way— it latches itself onto your dreams and goals; subtly slowing your momentum. If the problem is not addressed in a timely manner, Doubt, then deploys the emergency brakes to prevent all forward motion. No forward progress equals no motion. No advancement towards your goals means that the dream dies. Doubt succeeds.

Doubt's power comes from his ability to attack both internally and externally through personal interactions and environmental circumstances. Internally, he changes your vision and assessment of yourself. Rather than seeing the gifts, abilities, and stamina God has given you; Doubt causes you to focus on all your mistakes, the things you do not have, and the possibility of failure. Unlike conversations with others that begin and end, Doubt utilizes a much more dangerous weapon— your mind. Doubt can issue an unrelenting onslaught of depressing, anxiety-inducing thoughts that play in your mind day and night. Similar to the 3D view of plays during a professional football game, Doubt shows potential failures in 3D AND IN SLOW MOTION. He wants you to absorb it all.

Simultaneously, Doubt forces you into external interactions with people that result in them negatively assessing your dreams. These opinions usually come from those who continually remind you of how many times others have failed when they tried something similar. Additionally, Doubt brings people into your life who want to prevent you from succeeding— because they would prefer you stay where you are. These encounters attack your emotions, your thoughts, and ultimately your enthusiasm for the dream. Any combination of these can cause your dream to succumb to Doubt— ultimately destroying your dream.

Please understand that all endeavors are not a match for everyone, and there is such a thing as constructive criticism; however, the goal is to help you identify, bypass, and defeat the tactics of Doubt. First, you must identify those God-given dreams that you are made to achieve. These are the life, and sometimes, world changing dreams that Doubt does not want to come to pass.

Although the external attacks can be devastating, the internal attacks can be lethal. These take the wind out of your sails and the fuel out of your engine. Internal attacks cause you to doubt your own ability and to question every decision you have made, are making and ever will make. When you succumb to these attacks, you become unproductive causing your dreams to be taken off of life support. It is at this point that Doubt drains all hope, all inspiration, all aspiration, and all energy towards obtaining your dream.

***Tactics of Assassin #2***
This assassin is deadly. Do not take him for granted. Be ready to deal with him at any point in the pursuit of your dream. Doubt usually presents himself with unfounded ideas, images, thoughts, second-guessing, and an attitude of defeatism. He plays "heavy handed" and comes well-armed. He seems to understand all your insecurities. If we consider our faith to be the key ingredient of our success, Doubt would be its antithesis.

The symptoms of being infected by Doubt's weapons of choice are:

> ➢ Your speech changes in such a way that every comment you make questions your ability to achieve your goal.
>
> You begin to say:
>
>> "I'm not smart enough."
>>
>> "What was I thinking to embark on this journey?"
>>
>> "Who was I kidding?"
>>
>> "I'm such a failure."
>>
>> "I don't have the opportunities everyone else has."

- You no longer "see" yourself successful or achieving your dreams.

    Your thoughts include:

    > "I have never seen anyone else like me make it so who am I kidding? There's no way for someone like me to do this."

    > "This dream involves too much work. I can't see myself working that hard."

    > "I cannot imagine myself making that much money."
    > "There are so many people smarter than me. How can I lead them?"

- You believe every negative comment ever said about you.

    Doubt is so good at his job, that he reminds you of comments from decades ago.

    > "You are not smart."

    > "You do not have the right experience."

    > "You don t' know the right people."

"You had average grades in high school. What makes you think you can succeed now?"

"You didn't even go to college."

"You don't have any money for that."

➢ You begin to count the costs of all that has been done to date, and you question whether it was worth it.

"I invested so much time, but it was not recognized."

"So much money was invested in the last venture, and it failed. I can't do it again."

"I put so much effort into the growth of my employees, but they keep leaving. It isn't worth the effort anymore."

"Look what I've done so far, and I've had poor results."

When Doubt realizes one or more of these tactics is working, his next step is usually to use what I call the "snowball effect." The "snowball effect" is when he realizes one tactic is working, so he relentlessly piles on one to two more until they take root. Once that happens, he rapidly piles on as many additional tactics, until it becomes a giant "snowball" that is difficult to stop as it increases its downhill momentum. This is a very real phenomenon that pushes down your dreams and goals. Stopping that momentum before it picks up speed needs to be your top priority.

Let's say that your dream is to start a business. You've done preliminary research on the market that you're aspiring to enter, you're making connections within the field, and you've even started telling people about your business venture— you're making good progress; this is when Doubt comes in and begins to whisper negative thoughts in your mind. "Are you sure you're smart enough to take on this task?" "You've met so many people in the field. Why haven't you found an investor?" "Did you make the right decision?" These seemingly small questions begin to shake the foundation that you've built. Doubt will continue to whisper these negative questions day and night, without relenting. As you begin to second guess yourself, Doubt will then introduce you to people— who may even be within your field— who will cause you to take a step back from your dream. They may ask questions like, "Are you sure about that?" "Maybe you should look for a traditional job." "So-and-so tried the same thing three years ago, but their company failed." These questions, allowed to take root, serve as a one-two punch to your dreams.

Another tactic used by this Assassin that needs to be noted, is his propensity to invite other Assassins. Unlike assassins in films— hired guns who usually work alone— this one loves to invite others with varying skillsets to destroy your dreams. When they team up, the result can be a person who suffers from depression, insecurities, lack of motivation, and ultimately, a lack of purpose. All these impact a person's quality of life.

### Strategies to Thwart the Tactics of Assassin #2

At this point, Doubt has done his job and chalks it up as a victory for himself. The truth is far different though— he cannot win unless you allow him to win. You must remember it is never over unless God says it is over. Do you remember the Biblical account of Jesus' friend, Lazarus? This friend became ill and eventually died. His life, his plans, and his hopes seemed to have ended once he breathed his last breath. The hopes of his family members also seemed to have died as time passed. But Jesus, arriving at the appointed time, called life back into Lazarus. At that moment, what seemed like a lost cause became full of hope and expectation. New life was breathed back into both Lazarus' plans, and the hopes of his family. That's why it's not over until God says it is over.

Doubt believes that because he has such a long record of accomplishment, that you will give up and not fight back. He believes you will not pay attention to what God says. Do not give in nor allow Doubt to dictate what he will do to you. You need to tell him what you will do to him!

The Biblical account of David and Goliath is another good illustration for what we are discussing. You see, size and bark do not matter. If you have a good idea or dream, you should ask yourself, "Why not me"? When Goliath came and challenged the army of Israel, the experienced men hid and became afraid. In their minds, Goliath had such a strong track record of success against formidable enemies, that Israel didn't stand a chance. David, on the other hand, didn't worry about his age or size when confronting Goliath. In fact, Goliath was much bigger (estimates up to 9' 9" or ~297cm) and more experienced at fighting than David. Goliath shouted all types of threats and insults about what he was going to do to Israel and David. He also reminded them of the countless others who tried to come against him and failed. The remarkable thing was, his threats did not phase David. In David's mind, none of it mattered since he knew his dream, and no one was going to take it from him. When the threats did not work, Goliath decided it was time to engage the boy David in battle. While that is interesting, what happened next was crucial— David didn't wait and take the defensive approach in hopes of "surviving." Instead, he took the offensive and attacked the enemy armed with only a slingshot and stones. Unexpected to say the least!

Doubt is a lot like Goliath— seemingly insurmountable, unbeatable, or even invincible. However, much like in the David and Goliath case, Doubt can be beaten.

If you want to destroy this assassin and achieve your dream, you need to utilize the following strategies:

1. Attack the Assassin – in order to attack an enemy in front of you, there must be confidence that you can win. Confidence and assurance of outcome does not leave room for Doubt. Taking the offensive causes this Assassin to slow his forward progress while he assesses what it is you are doing. During his moment of hesitation, you need to fill yourself with confidence that you can win. First, read the Bible and see what God says about your situation. You will find many scriptures that affirm you have everything you need through Christ (Rom. 8:37; Mark 9:23; Phil. 4:13).

2. Get the Vision – it is important that you see yourself winning and achieving. The more you see yourself victorious, the more you want to drive forward until it becomes a reality. Most world-class athletes see themselves succeeding in their sport before it actually happens. Those that run track see

themselves crossing the finish line before the beginning of the race. Successful running backs see themselves scoring a touchdown before the play begins. Grab the vision and make it a part of your everyday life.

3. Study – understand the "playing field." Spend time researching what is needed to reach your goal. No matter how large the task may seem, remember steps 1 and 2. Study the resources needed, the approvals necessary for your vision to become reality, and study various strategies used in the past so that yours can be more refined and successful.

4. Enjoy the baby steps – although your vision may be grand, acknowledging and enjoying each small step along the road infuses confidence, excitement and joy during your journey. These ingredients will push you from one phase to the next until you reach your goal.

5. Talk – practice talking about your vision. It does not matter if you talk to the mirror or another human. You need to hear yourself speaking with confidence about what you

are doing. Can you hear the excitement in your voice? Can you clearly talk about it so that even you understand your goal? Can you convince yourself how awesome it will be? Be confident in what you are doing so that it translates to your conversations.

These strategies will help you move forward while destroying the tactics of the assassin named Doubt. Although Doubt can be powerful, he is no match for you if you follow the strategies outlined above. Most of all, hold on to strategy #1 and realize that you can do all things through Christ!

# Chapter Three
## Assassin #3 – Distraction

The next Assassin that will be introduced, lays such a subtle and effective trap, that most people have fallen into it without knowing how. Think about your "to do" list over the past week. If you are like most people, you have a list of tasks you want to complete by the end of the week. Throughout the week you may complete a few tasks here and there; but more often than not, every task doesn't get completed. At the end of the week, when you realize how many tasks you still have left to do; you may ask yourself, "What happened? How come I didn't accomplish most of what I wanted to?" In most cases, the answer to that question, is the Assassin, "Distraction". Distraction causes most people to become busy and engaged in a great deal of activities, but oftentimes, those activities have nothing to do with the original goals and plans that were set for the week. When this occurs, it's easy to just throw your hands up in the air or to blame it on life; but in actuality it is more of an indication that Assassin #3 is on the prowl.

This particular Assassin is cunning, deliberate, and focused on destroying any dream you hold dear. When this Assassin steps onto the battlefield of your life, he has no intention of leaving until he wins— or if you force him to submit! You see, going to war with Distraction is not for the impatient; but, for those who will not rest until this enemy is defeated and their dream realized. If you are a person who does not like to exert much energy or confront issues, then you will have a difficult time defeating this Assassin. Even the faint of heart needs to stand up to Distraction and let him know that you are strong and more than a conqueror!

There are many who would agree that Distraction is running rampant in the lives of countless people today. He seems to be everywhere— never discriminating between the young and old, male or female, rich or poor. His mission is clear— waylay you from achieving your dreams— and, over the years, he has become a formidable foe. With that said, please know that he *can* been defeated. You can win this battle and emerge victorious. You must win!

In the current world we live in, the "have it my way" mindset is running rampant. This impatient, "I want it now" mindset places finishing tasks and goals low on the totem pole of priorities. We must be of the mindset that the good works we put our "hands" to must be followed through until the expected end is reached. This book is a good example of the war with Distraction and reaching the final victory. You see, I began the journey of writing this book in 2012, but early in the process, Distraction was winning. My dream of completing this book was often on life support. There were many distractions— ministry, business, family and a host of other things— that interfered with my focus. Distraction had its grip on my dream— so much that it was gasping for air! Fortunately, focus, revitalization and inspiration were infused into this dream so that I was able to complete this book and defeat this Assassin.

**Tactics of Assassin #3**
Much like the other Assassins, Distraction has many weapons; but there are a few weapons of choice that he frequently uses. Let's take a moment and examine these weapons so that you can understand what you are fighting.

> ➤ Examination — All of us face distractions at various times throughout our lives; but have you noticed that every distraction seems specifically tailored to counter what you are trying to accomplish? I have noticed over the years that all distractions are not created equal. It's as if Distraction tailors each attack to the right duration and intensity so that it will knock our dreams off course. In other words, each attack is designed to test your fortitude and determination— will you keep pressing forward or will you quit? It is a test to see how much you actually want this dream to become reality.
>
> Look at it this way: Many of you were involved in high school athletics to varying degrees. For those of you who participated

in track and field, you know that for middle- and long-distance races, the winners often come down to one thing— who wants to win more. Who will push through the fatigue and continue until they cross the finish line first? When I was in high school, I ran track. There were many times while running the 400 meters my fortitude and endurance were tested. At that point, my body was usually screaming, "enough already!" With the finish line in sight and my body tired, I had a couple of options— give up or push myself. Even though I heard my body "talking," I had to ignore it and push until I crossed the finished line. If I didn't, I never would have reached my personal goals. This is key in learning how to counter Distraction's attacks.

When Distraction examines your fortitude, will he find a deep well of determination or a puddle? Will the depth of your fortitude and determination make him reconsider attacking you, or will he assume you are a "push over" because he doesn't see any form of resistance? It is not a matter of "if" this Assassin will appear in your life, but "when" will he appear. I understand that we live in a 24 hours-a-day news and entertainment cycle. I also understand that emails, social media, and other avenues of communication can distort our focus; but you need to examine your fortitude and build it up, if necessary.

- Time Avalanche — Time, or the misuse of it, is one of Distraction's favorite tools. This tool is very effective and often lands a disorienting blow to the dream seeker. Most people face this every week if not every day. At this point you may be thinking, "What is a time avalanche?"

Have you ever set a timeframe for completing a task or goal? After the timeframe was set, did you find your time being eaten away by smaller, less important things? Was your attention diverted? Did it affect your goals? If you've answered "yes," then you've experienced a time avalanche. Essentially, the way Distraction uses a time avalanche is by allowing you to set a timeframe for completing your task or dream— whether you have thoroughly thought through the timing or not is irrelevant. Once the timeframe is set, Distraction sends small "Time Stealers" to eat the time you've allotted to work toward your dream. Once your attention has been diverted— even "briefly"— and you say, "I can still make it," Distraction sends more "Time Stealers." These "Time Stealers" may even be noble and worthy efforts, but they do not need to be completed right at that moment— although you initially think they do.

"Time Stealers" are any activity that drain the allotted time you have set aside for achieving your dream. For example, you determine that you want to paint your bedroom a specific color (the goal) and decide that you can get the project completed on an upcoming Friday and Saturday (the Time). In order to achieve the goal, you decide to go to the home improvement store to buy the necessary supplies. However, while you are at the store, you notice they have a storewide sale for outdoor equipment and supplies. At that moment, you decide you want to build a patio (Time Stealer). The materials are dirt cheap— but this turns your 30-minute trip into a four-hour adventure. Before leaving the store, you decide to purchase all your supplies and have them delivered by Friday afternoon. The delivery comes as expected and you spend a couple of hours outside with the delivery person (Time Stealer), then you decide to position all the supplies. On Saturday morning, you decide to begin some of the prep work for the patio (Time Stealer) before coming inside to begin to paint the room. At this point, you will not complete painting the bedroom because other activities have devoured your time. These are "Time Stealers".

Distraction usually piles on these "Time Stealers" once he knows they are working. In my case, Distraction piled on numerous "Time Stealers" in order to delay my dream— publishing this book— for several years. When "Time Stealers" have success, they often delay other dreams and goals that were queued. We must be attentive to this and address it right away.

> Alternative Overload — I have often believed that having options is a good thing. When it comes to driving, it is often good to know alternative paths to take in the event of a traffic jam. Each time I have traveled from the Washington, D.C. area past Richmond, Virginia, I always factor in alternative routes because there is a high likelihood of a traffic jam throughout the trip. Alternately, these days, there are numerous apps that help us navigate the highways in hopes of finding the shortest distances to our destination.

Distraction will try to *overload you with alternatives*, making it difficult to discern which is the best option. For many, they become paralyzed because they now have too many options. In other words, there is a lack of understanding regarding what is the best option, allowing fear— of making the wrong choice— to creep in.

If you have ever traveled the highways, you know that in certain areas, you may see numerous signs that supposedly take you to the same place. I know in Florida, when I travel on I-4, there are multiple exits that are supposed to take you to Orlando. I used to ask myself, "which is the best one to take?" The answer was always, "It depends." If I had succumbed to the Alternative Overload, I would come to a complete stop on I-4 because I wouldn't know which was the best option. Of course, that would be dangerous!

The Assassin, Distraction, loves to overload you with numerous options and then ask you to choose the correct door. Is the correct option behind door #1, door #2 or door #3? You need to be aware and not let it overload you.

➢ Exhaustion — This is one of Distraction's preferred weapons to use against you. From Distraction's perspective, if he can get you involved in as many "Time Stealers" as possible, he knows you will become tired and possibly exhausted. When this happens, all forward progress stops. When you stop, you often stop dreaming, thus killing or impairing your current dream while also delaying or destroying future ones. Most people begin their initial pursuit of their dreams with a sprint and forget to pace themselves. Without pacing yourself and adhering to your schedule, you become exhausted and discouraged.

Exhaustion not only relates to your physical state, but also your mental state. When "Time Stealers" are continually nipping at your dreams and you entertain them, eventually they will take up an exorbitant amount of energy and time. In many cases, sleep will be deprived, rest becomes a distant memory, and your mind continues to race all day and night. After days and weeks of convincing yourself that you are okay, you eventually realize that you are exhausted. Once again, everything comes to a stop. All of this is a result of focusing on the things that are not helpful in achieving your dream.

➢ Opinions — This may be a sensitive topic; but have you noticed that people always have opinions about everything? Since the internet— and more specifically, social media— has provided a voice to everyone; there is the expectation that everyone should have a voice in everything. Unfortunately, this way of thinking is not healthy. When it comes to your plans and dreams, Distraction loves to encourage others to offer you their thoughts on what you are trying to accomplish. Oftentimes, negative comments prevail. No matter who you are, negativity can wear you down. When Distraction hurls enough of these opinions in your direction, it causes you to second guess every decision that you make— essentially making you ineffective. Those decisions you had already settled on, are now reopened. Please understand that it is not wrong to reassess your goal or project, but I am referencing the negativity generated from jealousy, pride, and people who are not visionaries.

As children, most of us have heard the expression, "Sticks and stones may break my bones, but words will never harm me." In many cases, this expression may be true; however, when Distraction finds a way for his weapon, Opinions, to penetrate your armor, it can cause just as much harm as being physically hit. When this happens, the words, opinions, and online reviews will impact your dream in more ways than you may realize.

***Strategies to Thwart the Tactics of Assassin 3***
1. Examination — This is an important step. When Distraction probes the depth of your fortitude and determination, you should also honestly examine yourself. Ask yourself if the dream you want to pursue is really your goal or just a passing fad? If it is a true goal, ask yourself if you are truly willing to make sacrifices in order to see it to completion? This means you are committed to pursuing this dream no matter how long it takes. If you have asked yourself these questions and you are willing to put in the time and effort, then get ready for Distraction to examine your fortitude; and get ready to let him know that you are going to win this battle. Remember, he plays the "long game" so you must show that you are willing to play to win.

    As you progress, continue to monitor your determination. Be determined to continuously examine where you are on your timeline; and be willing to make corrections where necessary. Fight through each changing emotion as they present themselves and stay focused on the goal. Remember to tell yourself that you **will** continue until you see the expected end!

2. Time Avalanche — This is more of a warning: Do not get caught in the Time Avalanche! You see, avalanches are both quick and devastating. Once they appear, you only have a moment to get out of its way. You must remember to manage your time wisely— be very protective of it! If you allot 5 hours per week on your dream, make sure you guard those 5 hours. Do not let the "Time Stealers" get a foothold in your life; assess— either daily or weekly— your progress. You will have to learn how to politely say "no" to "Time Stealers" when you are pursuing your dream. It is okay to be generous with the time not allotted for working towards your dream but keep the time separate.

3. Alternative Overload — This is a simple weapon to defeat **IF** you are deliberate in your focus. After you have set your goal and you begin planning to push forward, determine what is most important in your journey. Decide who needs to travel with you on this journey and where the journey is headed. Other criteria should be applied that are specific to your dream pursuit. Once you know them, apply them to all the alternatives and then select the correct one. Continue to pursue that direction until you reach your goal or there is a strong reason for change.

4. Exhaustion — Balance is the key to defeating this weapon. A wise man once said, "to everything there is a season" (Eccl. 3:1). To prevent exhaustion, you need to understand when you should rest, and when you should push forward. For instance, I have read that Albert Einstein slept for 10 hours a day. He knew when to sleep and when to work. We must understand that when we are exhausted— usually due to pursuing "Time Stealers"— we are no good to our dream. Our quality of work decreases. Do not let that happen.

5. Opinions — We must learn to develop both thick skin and a filter. Developing thick skin will help to protect from all the verbal opinions sent our way; while developing a filter will make sure that we only listen to what is helpful, rather than destructive. We should continually review, visualize, and monitor our plans; this allows us to know whether we have addressed everything needed to meet our expected goal, or if we have missed something.

*"Wise decisions are not influenced by favoritism."*

# Chapter Four
## Assassin #4 – Favoritism

Have you heard of this Assassin? Have you ever thought about this particular Assassin causing you to miss your destiny and blessing? Believe me, it has more of an impact than most people realize. Favoritism's goal is to cause you to miss your blessing, and to miss your appointed time of success. In other words, this Assassin's goal is to cause you to take a wrong turn and miss the movement of God.

I understand that some of you may not be convinced but let me highlight a couple of scenarios.

Scenario A
*A number of years ago, on a Saturday morning, my wife and I decided to go out to a restaurant for breakfast. While there, we discussed our need for a new car and the types of cars we would be interested in purchasing. At this stage in our marriage, I still had the car I purchased at the end of my college years. My small, 3-cylinder car had seen its last days and we were both interested in replacing it for a "real" car. Being that we were interested in buying a new car, we made an impromptu decision to go to a local car dealership*

*in an affluent area— the problem was we were dressed in very casual attire. When we arrived at the dealership, the first salesperson literally ignored us because he made an assumption about our ability to purchase a vehicle solely based on our attire. However, a second salesman saw us, and immediately greeted us. We worked with that salesman and purchased a new car. The first salesman seemed shocked and disappointed because he let a commission walk past him. He lost his opportunity based on assumptions. He favored people who were dressed a certain way. The amazing thing was during the entire time we were at the dealership, no other customer came to him. He lost his opportunity for a commission.*

<u>Scenario B</u>
*In corporate America, I encountered numerous situations where hiring managers only wanted applicants from specific schools. There are some cases where, depending on the type of work a corporation conducts, it may make sense to favor candidates from specific schools. In my experience however, I have found that "a school does not make the perfect candidate." In my corporate roles, I have hired many candidates from prestigious schools, only to discover that they weren't great employees. I then realized that the great employees were those who wanted to learn, who were proactive, and cared about the success of the project and corporation. It was never based purely on the school. I learned not to show favoritism*

*based on the school, thus hiring the "right" candidate and not the "favored" one.*

Some of you may say, "C'mon, everyone shows favoritism," and unfortunately, you are correct. However, that does not diminish the impact of this Assassin. The more it is employed, the greater the chance that you will not be all you can be, nor will you reach the heights destined for you. Favoritism convinces you that benefits and blessings only come in certain "packages."

Over the course of my secular management career, I have been told that people make assessments of others within the first two minutes of introduction. I have seen this in action, and I must admit, I have also fallen prey to this. Fortunately, I have been willing and able to "snap out" of that way of thinking. In the Bible, Nathanael was prejudiced against Jesus— can you believe that? — when he found out Jesus came from a town called Nazareth. When he was told about Jesus of Nazareth in John 1:46, his question was, "Can anything good come out of Nazareth?" Wow! What a discriminatory statement.

You see, Nathanael had a certain, derogatory opinion about those in Nazareth; and he preferred **anyone** other than a Nazarene. Because of this, he almost missed the greatest blessing he could have experienced. Favoritism almost achieved his goal in Nathanael's life. Fortunately for Nathaniel, Phillip convinced him to come and meet Jesus, and Nathanael was forever changed!

Within the Church, we see Favoritism invading the relationships and interactions of members and visitors alike. I am certain you have experienced it also. For example:

    a. Many will ONLY listen to one style of Praise or Worship music.

    b. Many will ONLY listen to a message if the Senior Pastor delivers it. If someone else is scheduled to minister, they are conveniently absent.

    c. Some will ONLY listen to a message IF it is of a certain time length or fits into a particular format. For some, even fifteen minutes is too long!

    d. For some, they only receive messages as truth as long as the person delivering it looks like them. This could be ethnicity, dress attire, alma mater, economic status, tradition, or any other filter.

The examples mentioned above are just a sampling, and I am certain that you can think of many more. The problem with allowing Favoritism to filter your view, is that you can easily miss what the Lord is doing at this phase of your life. You must remember that gifts come wrapped in many different shapes and sizes: some are wrapped in square boxes, some in rectangular boxes, some with bows, and some without. One size does not fit all when it relates to your blessings and your destiny.

There is an account of a person who had to learn this the hard way. In Numbers 22, we read about Balaam— a wicked prophet. There was a message of warning directed to him, but it came in the most unexpected "package"— a donkey. It was a donkey who was trying to save him and warn him of the certain destruction ahead. It was not until the Lord allowed an unprecedented event to occur, that Balaam realized the message. The donkey spoke and told him about the angel in front of him with his sword drawn. If Balaam had not come to his senses in time, he would have died. It took a message from a donkey to make Balaam realize that the Lord can get life-saving messages to him through many different avenues.

This story shows us that the Assassin, Favoritism, blinds us from the truth. He wants us to believe that ONLY through a particular framework can success and destiny be achieved. The problem with this type of thought is that the framework we think should be used, may not be based on God's Truth. Without being based on His Truth, you can never reach the fullness of the success that He has for you.

Take a moment and assess whether this Assassin has taken a position in your life. Have you missed the mark? Have you allowed Favoritism to make you choose people or opportunities based on assumptions that have no basis? Have you used a baseless framework that caused you to make unprofitable decisions? When we examine our life, we are bound to find examples of times that this has happened.

***Tactics of Assassin #4***
As we discussed in the previous paragraphs, Assassin #4 designs his approach in a way that causes you to be blinded by qualities that have nothing to do with God's will in your life. When blinded, your destiny and your blessings are delayed or missed. Because of the subtly of how he attacks you, it may not be noticed that you have missed God's best for you until it is too late. When you miss God's best, you are often left with the question, "Why did this happen to me?"

In order to properly identify when Favoritism is in operation, examine your life to see if any of the following are operating in your life:

> ➢ When people enter your life, you assess them exclusively on their clothing, their car, their economic status, their educational background, etc. You may assume that because a candidate comes from an Ivy League school, they must be the best

candidate for the job; or you may assume that because a company had a role in a big movie production, that they would be a great asset on your Indie film. Assumptions like these are the result of Favoritism. These are a few examples of many where we allow Favoritism to make unwise decisions for us. Just because a person was involved in a major project, does not mean they are the right person for your project. In fact, although their name may have been mentioned, their role may have been almost nonexistent. Be careful of Favoritism, because this Assassin will cause you to make unwise decisions based on non-important and fleeting qualities. Clothing can be changed daily, industry names can be thrown around, and past experiences are only valuable when it directly relates to the upcoming project at hand. Do not fall for these qualities that Favoritism tries to convince you are the key components to your decision.

➢ Favoritism attempts to confine your acceptance and understanding of supporting detail and insight needed to make decisions. If a Pastor is attempting to decide whether to open a church in a certain location, but the one successful ministry he knows never opened a church in this type of neighborhood, his decision may be to bypass the neighborhood in need because his only definition of success is to follow the exact pattern of another ministry. In this scenario, he may miss the entire purpose God has for him and the church, and Favoritism would have succeeded once again.

➢ Cronyism is a tool loved by Favoritism. By definition, cronyism is the practice of partiality especially in awarding jobs or perks to friends, relatives or trusted colleagues. In this classic weapon of Favoritism, cronyism pushes the thought of hiring friends, family and trusted colleagues to positions of authority without regard to their qualifications or skillset. In a small, family-owned business, this may be okay but in a larger organization, this could be a recipe for disaster and often causes an organization to miss its goals. All of us are born with different skillsets, and depending on our desires, we can learn many others. Unfortunately, Favoritism clouds our judgment and our ability to objectively assess the skills needed to function in various roles. There are those who do not want and are not designed to sit behind a desk every day. Therefore, it would not make sense for that person to be given a job as a Vice President that calls for him to be in meetings all day, every day. How much progress would the company make when the newly appointed V.P. misses numerous meetings because "that isn't his thing?" For the sake of your organization, your church, your business, make appropriate decisions devoid of cronyism, but full of Godly wisdom.

### Strategies to Thwart the Tactics of Assassin 4

When making any decision, recognize that Favoritism is aggressively trying to influence and impair your decision-making process. Knowing this, please remember to use the following strategies to thwart his tactics:

1. If you are intent on making a decision in your life, be sure you understand the criteria for which you are making the decision. Are your criteria in line with God's will for your life and the strategic plan of the organization? Are your decisions based on the right moves, or are they based on your buddy's influence? Do you understand your need at the moment; and will the decision you are about to make fulfill that need? Remember to ask the Lord for guidance. He will give us direction, but we must remember to listen!

2. Do not confine your thinking and limit it to pre-conceived notions. Consider whether it

is possible that your organization, in route to its goals, may have to take a deliberate turn in order to properly align itself to the finish line. If so, include that thinking in your decision making. Do not limit the possibilities unless the current situation requires it. Make sure you understand the season and time you are in. Is it time for bold risks or limited choices? You must know this answer.

3. Cronyism is a terrible way to run an organization, whether it is a church or a business. It is a sure way to dampen the morale of others who are following you. On the other hand, if the strategic plan calls for the training of family, friends or trusted colleagues, and placing them in those positions when they are ready, that may not be a bad plan. Whatever your decision, just know that success does not come from people who look and act like you. Success is increased by those who have the qualifications you are objectively searching to find. When making personal decisions, make sure it is in line with your personal goals and objectives. Just because someone you know looks the part and made a similar decision to the one you anticipate making, you should do further research to ensure it is not "smoke and mirrors."

# Chapter Five
## Assassin #5 – Lust

In this chapter, we unveil one of the most lethal assassins out of the group— Lust. As lethal as he is, this Assassin is often unidentified or misidentified. The reason he continues to fly under the radar is because his attacks are veiled under the guise of "normal." Most people do not have an objection to what he does, nor his tactics. My hope is during this chapter, we can identify who he is, why he is dangerous, and how to thwart his tactics.

First, we must remember that everyone has a purpose in their life. No matter your status, the Lord has a purpose for you— you were not designed to be a carbon copy of the celebrities in Hollywood. One of each of them is enough. If you are serious about pursuing and living your God-given purpose, you need to be prepared to battle and defeat this Assassin. Additionally, you need to gain discernment so that you know when this Assassin is in operation.

Lust is the Assassin that causes you to look more at the physical rather than the entire picture. Lust, who often brings along his friend, Jealousy, pushes you to want what someone else possesses. Be aware: there is no limitation to what Lust desires. It could be someone else's car, spouse, career, home, hairstyle, clothes, position, etc. The key problem with this Assassin is that he is never satisfied. Once he convinces you to get one thing, you tire of it and want something else simply because you see someone with it.

Please understand that I am not suggesting you never enjoy the pleasures of life, but they must not become the god of your life. Specifically, this particular Assassin emboldens the desire to have what others have regardless of whether it is right for you. Because you see someone else with it, you suddenly desire to have it also. In many cases, Lust causes you to want what the admired person has or something very similar, regardless of timing or your ability to handle it. You find yourself living your life based on another person's life. No originality or creativity can exist in that scenario.

When living another person's life, you make assumptions about what you will like and what will make you happy solely based off of a mental filter that highlights the thing you covet. When it comes to finding "**the**" person to date or marry, often people look at Hollywood celebrities to determine the type of boyfriend or girlfriend they are hoping to find. We must understand the life of the rich and famous is not always as it seems.

Let's use kids as an example. If anyone has ever been around children, you know their wants and desires change rapidly. Many children constantly approach their parents with many questions and propositions. They usually sound something like this: "If you buy me this, I won't ask for anything else again." Does that sound familiar to anyone? Based on a commercial, television program, or a conversation with their friends, that item has now become something they "must have." The more they hear about it, the more they want it. It becomes their number one focus!

I recall an account when my daughter was younger, where she wanted a leather jacket. This jacket was waist length, at best; it was not thick by any means, but it was fashionable. After pleading to me on many occasions, I relented and allowed her to purchase the jacket. At first, she was so happy, but then a problem occurred. You see, she wore that jacket but she couldn't get warm. The reason was because it was winter time! That fashionable jacket became less desirable because my daughter was freezing every day. Finally, she stopped wearing it because it was not practical during sub-freezing temperatures. In this instance, Lust convinced my daughter that she must have the jacket. No thought went into whether it made sense to wear the leather jacket in winter.

The other lie that Lust spews is, "You will be happy once you have that item." People fall for that line of thinking all the time. They may even already be happy in life, but Lust gives them the impression that what they are currently experiencing is not true happiness. It causes them to chase after something that does not truly have substance. Finding happiness in things will always lead to disappointment.

Remember, Lust operates heavily in the visual realm. What I mean is, Lust leverages images and video to connect with his prey— he reaches all our senses in order to provide as real of a scenario as possible. It's the ultimate "this could be you" scenario— it's the perfect trap. Even before there were 4K video cameras, he produced the most realistic images. This attention to detail causes people to think whatever he is showing is better than what they already possess; and when a person takes the bait, he triggers their emotions— causing them to lose control over their emotions. in other words, emotions rule over the Truth.

The ultimate outcome of allowing Lust to rule is the demise of your dream and destiny. The reason this outcome can occur is because your passion now focuses on the object of your lust rather than completing your destiny. The decisions that need to be made are no longer made in a clear and timely manner. Rather than focusing on the end result, the focus becomes short-term until the focus is lost completely.

I've seen talented people take over an organization and offer a focused plan and destination. In one case, all went well until he allowed Lust to cause him to focus on another man's wife. Once that relationship became heated, everything else began to crumble. He no longer led as he once did, and the organization suffered. Eventually, he had to resign— not only did his dreams at that organization die, but two marriages crumbled, and families were damaged. Lust won.

**Tactics of Assassin #5**
This Assassin loves to blind you, snatch up your emotions, and entangle you in a web of deceit and unhealthy urges. Lust has caused the downfall of countless prominent people over the generations— even going as far back as Biblical times. If he had success during the Biblical times and in generations since, you must realize that he is good at what he does and therefore, do not underestimate him. With that being said, do not drop your guard; and remember that with God, all things are possible.

Some of the most common tactics used by this Assassin are as follows:

> ➤ Lust gives you the premise that no matter what you have, it is never enough. To be clear, I am not saying that you should not improve and strive to go higher in life; I am saying that Lust wants you to think your possessions are insufficient. Remember, Eve fell into this trap in the Garden of Eden.

When the serpent approached her and told her that she would have the knowledge of Good and Evil if she ate of the tree, she did not even stop to think, "Wait. I have it good already. Why would I want to know evil? I am not lacking anything." Instead, she followed the serpent's lead and assumed she was missing something. That is how Lust works today. If your church has 50 members and your friend's church has 700 members, you assume the larger church is better. Or, if you have a nice sports car and your friend's sports car has a more prestigious name, you assume his is better and you want it.

➤ "A little fire won't hurt you." This is the mantra that Lust wants you to live by. He wants you to dabble in areas that are not beneficial to your destiny or your health. Many assume that a little "fun" will not hurt, but later find out that following their Lust was the worst decision they could make. Whether you are addressing personal goals or organizational goals, dabbling in "fire" will always leave a mark. Rather than taking part in things that you know will hurt your progress, stay away from those things that aren't good for you and stay your course—time is important, and you cannot easily make up lost time. Remember, Lust's goal is to kill your dream by distracting you from your goal!

- Continue to gaze in the wrong direction. What I mean by gaze is to stare intently or deliberately. Gazing is great when you are focused on your goals, objectives, and destiny. If your focus is in a different direction, it can cause catastrophic problems. King David discovered this when Lust grabbed him and convinced him to look at another man's wife bathing on the roof. Normally, he would have been in battle with his men, but he stayed behind this time. With excess time on his hands, he used it unwisely and lusted after another man's wife— eventually committing a major sin. You can read the tragic outcome in 2 Samuel 11. Lust took King David's focus from running the country, to solely focusing on pursuing Bathsheba.

**Strategies to Thwart the Tactics of Assassin 5**
1. *No matter your station in life, learn to appreciate what you have.* You should always strive for better, but do not under-appreciate what you currently possess. Every staircase is built up of many steps; with each step you take, you get closer to your goal. Just remember that you are on one step of the staircase— which means

you are on your way up! Appreciate where you are, and let that appreciation continue to propel you upward. Do not get caught in the never-ending comparison battle of feeling like you must have whatever the "Joneses" purchase.

2. *Stay focused and determined*— there are many distractions and "opportunities" to go off course. In fact, Lust wants to provide the perfectly catered— although completely terrible— option for you to delay for progress. He knows that if he can delay you, his chances of entrapping you increase immensely. Once he has entangled you in his web, it is difficult— though not impossible— to free yourself and get back on track. Surround yourself with people who can positively contribute to your goals, and gaze constantly at the end result. Only engage in things that move you forward, not backwards. I heard a quote attributed to Les Brown that stated,

> *"The graveyard is the richest place on earth, because it is here, that you will find all the hopes and dreams that were never fulfilled."*

Do not let Lust put your destiny among this number.

3. *Always focus your gaze towards the end result.* Prior to each race, track and field athletes always picture themselves at the finish line. Once the starting pistol is fired, they always look forward. Can you imagine someone running the 110-meter hurdles while looking behind and to the side? It would end in disaster. He would fall, and possibly take others down with him. That is the same scenario when a person gives in to Lust's persuasion to look elsewhere. Ignore Lust, it can be single minded— in other words, destiny first!

*"Asking for help is not a display of weakness."*

# Chapter Six
# Assassin #6 – Pride

This agent of destruction is an obvious one but is often unaddressed. It is an agent that does not try to hide its presence, but it still seems to find its target and successfully eliminate it. The interesting part is he can easily be seen by others, although the one being attacked (the one suffering from his presence) may not notice. This Assassin does not discriminate based on ethnicity, religion, economics, gender or nationality. He is an equal opportunity predator.

Before we go any further, let's clarify what we mean by pride. I am not saying that you should not take pride in the work you do. In that sense, we should complete our work and have a sense of satisfaction or pride in the finished product. We should always want to do great work. Additionally, I am not saying you should not be proud of someone— like a parent is of their child. In that case, you are pleased with that person whether it is based on their performance, how they've grown or some specific event. All of these are good and natural opinions and emotions to possess.

This Assassin named Pride, is different than the aforementioned examples. He digs into your life with the goal of changing your heart. He wants you to hear his lies, begin to believe them, and thus, change your heart. You see, heart issues are extremely important to address. Whether your heart speaks of truths birthed from God's Word, or from the latest emotion or fad; you will become or achieve what your heart believes. If Pride convinces you to have an unrealistic view of yourself, your attention will be diverted. This will lead you ending up in an unhealthy place.

Solomon— known as the wisest man to ever live— shared about the impact of this Assassin. In Proverbs 16:18 (MSG) it says, *"First Pride, then the crash — the bigger the ego, the harder the fall."* Pride is that Assassin that provides an unrealistic assessment of oneself. He makes you believe the world revolves around you. Pride puffs you up with no substance or foundation underneath you for support. It pushes you up higher and higher until your support bursts like a balloon, and you fall back down to earth. Once Pride begins to change your heart and your view, he causes you to alienate others around you. Especially those who have helped you succeed up to this point.

The great news is: you can determine if Pride is invading your life. Once confirmed, aggressively push it out. Nothing good comes from it.

A few tips on how to recognize Pride's presence:

> ➢ Listen to your conversation. If everything is "I" and there is no "we" or "the team," begin

to wonder if you are taking all the credit when really it should be shared.

➢ Do you feel like success only comes if you do it? Even though others may be capable of completing tasks, do you find yourself dissatisfied if you are not the one who does the work?

➢ When you attend events, do find yourself criticizing it by saying, "I would do it this way...?"

These are a few indications that Pride is gaining a foothold in your life. Your God-given destiny and your full success depend on you identifying this Assassin and eradicating him before he impacts you.

Throughout the Bible, Pride is discussed with the Lord's view of it. In Proverbs 8:12-13, we find:

> 12 *"I, wisdom, dwell with prudence,*
> *And find out knowledge and*
> *discretion.*
> 13 *The **fear** of the LORD is to hate*
> *evil;*
> ***Pride** and arrogance and the evil*
> *way*
> *And the perverse mouth I hate."*

Here we see that Pride is the opposite of wisdom, prudence, knowledge, and discretion. Think about it for a minute. Everyone knows you need wisdom in order to succeed in life— specifically, Godly wisdom. If wisdom is connected to knowledge and God's ways, what does that say about Pride?

**Tactics of Assassin #6**
Pride, Assassin #6, is so prevalent through this world today that it is not "if" you may encounter him but "when." On any given day, you can see him operating and ruining the lives of many people. When examining Pride's tactics, we observe numerous methods of attack, however, we will only focus on a few of them:

> ➢ Pride loves to focus your attention on the accolades given to you by others. Every time someone tells you what a great job you have done, or how important you are to the job, he causes you to take every syllable and inflection to heart, such that you esteem yourself higher than you should. He helps you to "inflate" successful situations in your life; and causes Pride to rise up where your focus becomes me-myself-and-I. Do you have friends that like to recount "the game?" You know, a particular game in high school where he or she performed exceptionally well? It may have been the only game in the person's high school career that was a good memory but the inflation of every second of

that game and their role in it is shared with you every time you see them. Or, because someone was great in high school, they conclude that they should be competing at the professional level.

➢ Have you ever encountered people who believe they are always correct? You know, those people who cannot imagine ever being wrong about anything. If something does not agree with their conclusion, it must be the fault of someone else or the process. I have encountered many people who view themselves as perfect. Unfortunately, they do not realize there is no one perfect except the Lord Jesus. These are often people who have been controlled by Pride. They are blind to their own faults and only see the faults of others— they are people who walk around with blinders given to them by Pride, but they do not realize it. With the blinders on, they try to force you to prescribe to their way of thinking although their vision is limited. Pride has deep roots in these types of people, while humility is absent from their lives— all because they took the bait from Pride to believe they can do no wrong. Those who have fallen victim to this attack by Pride are in a dangerous place, because even with all of their "perfections," they cannot identify the holes in their strategies or the dangers in their life choices. Do not let Pride use this tactic on you.

➤ Because Pride loves to provide its victims with a lofty— or elitist— image of themselves, they often believe that everyone else is beneath them. Successfully planted in their lives, Pride causes the victims to develop a condescending attitude towards others. They believe a conversation with the average person is a waste of time, and beneath them. Once ingrained, these folks become untouchable, unapproachable, and un-relatable. Ultimately, they become out of touch with their mission and goals; and their teams become disengaged and unresponsive to the needs of the organization. Successes come at an increasingly distant interval.

➤ When Pride has been successful in the previously mentioned areas, he attempts to totally disconnect you from God. Those who enter this phase of a relationship with Pride encounter a dangerous point in their life. They are at a precipice without even realizing it— the life and death of dreams are in the balance. The decisions made at this stage may have a lasting impact. At this stage, the self-focus— self-importance— is so intense that they fall in love with what they see and call it "perfect!" Let me remind you that Lucifer fell into this trap himself. He looked inwardly, at his own uniqueness and his nearness to God, that he thought he was the most beautiful and worthy being. He thought he should be above God— yes, even God— even though God was the one who created him. When Pride is fully operating at this level in someone's life, logic no longer exists. Conclusions drawn by people in this state often make you wonder how they were able to come to a conclusion that makes no logical sense. I once knew a gentleman who had some military training and was happy with his physique. Because he thought so highly of himself, he decided he wanted to walk by himself through the roughest part of town to see if anyone would bother him. He assumed he could handle anyone. I don't know if he ever did it, but I do remember that Proverbs 16:18 reminds us that "Pride comes before destruction".

## *Strategies to Thwart the Tactics of Assassin #6*

1. The Tactics of Assassin #6 are known and defensible, but you must stay alert to what he is doing. In order to defeat this attack, learn to be gracious. It is okay for people to express their thankfulness to you for something you have done. In my roles as an Executive in several companies and as a Pastor of a church, I have often wanted to

award, appreciate, and express my gratefulness to people who have made good contributions in their roles. With that being said, appreciate the moment but don't inflate your ego to the point where you feel like your work is so much better than anyone else's. Learn to be good at the work you do and the effort you support, but do not do it just to receive accolades. Don't forget Prov 27:2, *"Let another man praise you, and not your own mouth; A stranger, and not your own lips."* Be excited that you have the ability to contribute to something good; and appreciate the opportunity to learn and to give of yourself to others. Be thankful that you were allowed to do something good.

2. Always remember that you do not know everything. If you have the understanding that you can always learn something through others, you will not limit your understanding to a finite number of people. Test your thoughts against the Word of God and increase your thinking; and keep a humble, but diligent spirit about you. When you listen to people from all walks of life, you begin to learn more, and you can become an asset to others.

3. Remember to have a realistic opinion of yourself. Do not think yourself higher than you should. It may be true that you are one

of the best business consultants around, but it does not mean you will win every bid. Be confident in your skillset, but not arrogant. Always have a thirst to get better but stay humble. Always remember that it is the Lord who allows you to experience success; and he really is the vine and we are the branches. All nourishment comes from the vine. If you operate with that in mind, Pride will not have a place in your life.

4. If you ever wanted to understand the proper relationship you should have with the Lord, always visit Psalm 42:1. Our relationship with God should always reflect an insatiable desire to be in His will. As the deer pants for water, we should always long for and value our relationship with the Lord. If He is in our lives, businesses, relationships, families, and everything else that concerns us, will be healthy. Even more, Pride will not be able to find an opening from which to operate. Additionally, he will not be able to cut our connection to the Lord, which means we can continue to focus on moving towards our destiny— the one created by the Lord for us. The fullness of the blessing He has for us can be experienced. Guard this relationship thoroughly.

*"Forgive so that you will not be imprisoned."*

# Chapter Seven
## Assassin #7 – Unforgiveness

This Assassin is good at what he does. It builds up subtly through the frequently open doors to your heart. These doors are often open to him because of a past trauma in your life, usually based on an event in a relationship. It is often caused by a perceived betrayal, or it can team up with Assassin #5 to provide a one-two punch. When Unforgiveness rolls into your life, his impact is subtle initially, but he continues to grow stronger at a rapid pace. This particular Assassin stops the flow of God in your life right away. If you want to see the works of God cease in your life, let Unforgiveness take a stronghold in your life.

Remember, God leads by example and He expects us to do the same. Clearly, forgiveness is the key to right alignment with God. In Matthew 18, Peter asked Jesus how many times he had to forgive a brother or sister that hurt him. Jesus shocked Peter and the other Disciples by saying "*seventy times seven.*" In other words, Jesus is implying that you should continually forgive. If forgiveness is intended to be that important in our lives, we must understand the Assassin Unforgiveness should not have a place in our lives. He is clearly pitching a different viewpoint than Jesus, therefore we should not listen or get comfortable with him.

The entirety of Jesus' earthly ministry featured forgiveness. Even at the Cross, He said, *"Father, forgive them for they know not what they do."* Think about it for a moment. While He was in excruciating pain—dying— He interceded on our behalf to ask for forgiveness. Why would He do that? Yes, Jesus does love us and that is the basis for this intercession, but something else is also at play. He wanted us to follow His example and forgive, because He knew that Unforgiveness would drag down our elevation to our ordained destiny. He knew that Unforgiveness would cause us to change our focus from our destiny and His will, thus focusing more on the incident and potential hatred of the person who wronged us.

Let me provide a different perspective for those who own businesses. All businesses should have a business plan inclusive of the vision and objective; and everything a business does should be in line with the plan. The intent is for the plan to lead the business towards its goals and objectives. I am certain that when you follow the plan, the organization does well. I am also certain that when your daily, weekly and monthly activities become misaligned with the goals, the company flounders. If sometime during the life of your company, a competitor steals an idea from you, the natural reaction is to get angry. I am sure you could say you will never forgive them for it— it is even understandable. However, if a company places too many resources and focus on retribution, they eventually lose their direction. The resources that could have been used for marketing, research, and development are now focused on inflicting harm to the offending company. It may feel good for a moment, but it will also cause you to lose time. While focusing exclusively on the competitor who stole from you, another competitor rises up and surpasses both of you.

Often when thinking about this Assassin, we assume that we are only referencing our relation to other people. A little known or acknowledged secret is this Assassin can cause you to be your biggest critic— actively highlighting all your failures and flaws. Once he has done that, he piles on the guilt to the point where you have trouble forgiving yourself. It is sometimes difficult to forgive others, but it is even more difficult to forgive yourself when you have reached this stage. Freedom, creativity, and success will only come once you have destroyed this Assassin. The weight that Unforgiveness places on you causes you to sink deeper and deeper into a never-ending abyss. This is the complete opposite of what God intends for you; so quickly let go of Unforgiveness!

**Tactics of Assassin #7**
As you can see, Unforgiveness is a lethal Assassin. In fact, many of you who are reading this book may realize this Assassin is in your life. Take his presence seriously and prepare to resist him. To that end, I wanted to highlight several tactics that

Unforgiveness uses in order to successfully derail or destroy your dream and destiny. This list is not all-inclusive, but a sampling of the most frequent tactics:

> ➤ Unforgiveness loves to approach you immediately after a person, or an organization does something that you perceive as a wrong towards you. Rather than objectively assessing what happened and strategizing how best to address the issue while continuing to perform according to your plan, you are convinced to focus most, if not all, of your energy and resources towards revenge. His goal is to prevent forward progress, by causing you to continuously review the incident in your mind from a standpoint of retaliation. All strategic planning and thought ends and only tactical planning remains. Tactical planning on a daily basis is good, but if you have lost your compass and direction, you cannot make forward progress.

> ➤ The weapons of this Assassin are very accurate. His favorite weapon causes you to focus heavily and almost exclusively on your emotions. When someone wrongs you and inflicts pain, Unforgiveness boldly steps into your life and zooms in to the emotional pain and anger experienced. He continues to amplify the negative emotions in such a way

that whenever the name of the person or organization is mentioned, the emotions of the incident rise inside of you— allowing you to relive the moment over and over.

➢ Added onto his prior weapons, Unforgiveness unleashes skepticism in our life so that we no longer trust others. Anyone who does not agree with you now appear on your "distrust list." As you go down this path, the number of friends and business partners begin to decrease because you push them away. Whether you realize it or not, no one can reach their full destiny and potential without interacting and depending on others. We do not live in a world of 7 billion islands. When you alienate yourself or your business, you are completely vulnerable to this Assassin.

➢ Assassin #7 does everything in his power to block your relationship with God. First, you must understand that any perceived success must come through God. Without Him, it is of no value. Knowing this, Unforgiveness aims to totally redirect your focus from God to the painful event. By doing so, you care more about Unforgiveness than anything or anyone else— Unforgiveness becomes your god. Instead of love, forgiveness, creativity, and success abiding in your life, you only have

Unforgiveness, revenge, hatred, and anger in your life. These are designed to block the flow of God in your life, thus only allowing you to listen to Unforgiveness. At this point, he has you spiraling out of control and down a pit of despair and depression. Because of his profound impact, he makes himself a comfortable space in your life with the intent to stay for a long time.

These tactics are frequently used by Assassin #7. Even though we know about his tactics, countless people still fall prey to him. As he gets rooted in the lives of many, including those within the Church, people often ask, "God, why is this happening to me?" Additionally, others ask, "Where is God in my situation?" We have to make sure we have not blocked Him out of our lives due to Unforgiveness.

**Strategies to Thwart the Tactics of Assassin #7**
Although the tactics of Unforgiveness have been deliberate and successful, we should not lose hope. We can defeat this Assassin and experience the destiny that God has for us. The guide below is simple, but do not underestimate the difficulty for some to do it. It requires a "denial of self" in order to realign yourself to God's will. These tactics will put you back on course towards your goals and destiny.

1. We are human and we do have emotions. The key point is not to let your emotions rule all your decisions. It may be true that someone did something to cause you harm, but in response you must not lose total focus on your goals and destiny. Press closer to the Lord. Ask for wisdom to know what to do next, and healing to address the pain caused by the offending party. Jesus tells us in Matthew 18:7 that "offenses must come." It is how we deal with these offenses that determine your success. If you are in business and another organization or person has caused you harm, address the issue but do not lose focus. Understand your vulnerabilities and address them, but double-down on your direction so that you can keep making forward progress.

2. Part of the blessing of being human are your emotions; however, conversely, part of the problem with being human are your emotions. You see, emotions can fluctuate from one end of the spectrum to the other. Without any parameters, emotions will take you to the highest heights one day and to the depths of the deepest pit the next day. Knowing this, we live with emotions, but all your decisions should not be emotion-based. God knows you have been hurt, but He wants you to know that He can heal all wounds. The wrong done to you or your

business could have caused emotional damage, but He wants you to know that He makes all things new! Instead of just focusing on the pain caused by the other party, focus on how you will still succeed and reach your goals. Envision your success despite the damage that someone else tried to inflict upon you. Rehearse that outcome over and over until you believe it. Remember that in Jesus, you can do all things.

3. I often think about the lessons Jesus taught us during His early ministry. One of His Disciples, Judas, who traveled with Him for over three years, betrayed Him for money. That betrayal must have hurt because although Jesus knew in advance what was going to happen, He still cared about the souls of every man and woman, inclusive of Judas. If Jesus approached the situation like many of us, He would never trust anyone again— especially those wanting to be the Treasurer! The betrayal would have sealed the fate of anyone wanting to interact with us. We would post big "Stay Away!" signs on the door to our hearts. Most of us would keep everyone at a distance no matter how sincere their intent; however, I want to encourage you to do something different. Let love prevail by still caring for and interacting with others. Examine yourself

and your processes to determine if there is something that needs to be changed in order to prevent these situations from reoccurring. You still need to forgive the offender, but you should not let them be your Treasurer going forward. Engross yourself with success. Look forward to interactions with other great people and organizations. Do not close yourself from the outside world. Move forward! Your experiences and success may be crucial to the well-being of many others.

4. I know in today's society, people belittle the importance of Jesus and our relationship to Him. But we should remember that our relationship to Him is paramount. He reminded us in John 15:5 that "without Me you can do nothing." Nothing means nothing! For us to live a great, well-rounded, and successful life, we must preserve our relationship with Him. Assassin #7 aims to take away the love that Jesus often preached about. Unforgiveness replaces love with hate, happiness with anger, and hope with pain. You need to push back on this Assassin and learn to "bless those who curse you, do good to those who hate you" (Matthew 5:44). Be determined to pursue His love in all that you do. In doing so, Unforgiveness will not have a means to turn

your heart away from God. He will not be able to destroy you nor your destiny.

# Chapter Eight
## Final Thoughts

Throughout this book, I wanted to highlight several Assassins that seem to wreak havoc in the lives of countless people. My goal was to highlight them and explain their impact in a straightforward and easy to understand manner. With this information, you should be able to defeat any of the Seven Dream Killers and achieve success. The only requirement is that you are honest with your self-assessment and the role these Assassins are currently playing in your life. Personally, I would love to see everyone who reads this book achieve great success and reach the destiny the Lord has set up for you— do not settle for less and do not get distracted. I believe that many people are depending on your testimony.

For those who are in business, I want to encourage you to stay close to Jesus and understand how His teachings can apply to your business practices. In a world where over 90% of startups fail, we need the percentage of successful businesses to increase beyond 10%. Take time to dream and thoroughly understand your vision; pray about it and let the Lord modify it for success. Refuse to entertain the 7 Dream Killers and understand that everything you have and will have comes from Him. Stay connected!

Finally, I want you to know that these Seven Dream Killers will attempt to attack you at various stages of your life. Therefore, you must always be on alert. I wrestled with Distraction for many years. For a period of time, he had the upper hand in my life. Due to his schemes, this book almost never made it from an idea, to a preached message, and finally, to this book. It took a time of focus and commitment to see this through. I believe you can also achieve your goals the same way. I eventually— through the help of the Lord— banished Distraction and moved forward towards my goal. I have learned that time is precious and it matters what we do with the time. My list of goals is still long so I know I must stay focused to reach them.

Will you do the same?

www.ingramcontent.com/pod-product-compliance
Lightning Source LLC
Chambersburg PA
CBHW050442010526
44118CB00013B/1640